# OUT-OF-THIS-WORLD ALIENS

## HIDDEN PICTURE PUZZLES

BY
JILL KALZ

ILLUSTRATED BY
SIMON SMITH

PICTURE WINDOW BOOKS
a capstone imprint

DESIGNER: LORI BYE
ART DIRECTOR: NATHAN GASSMAN
PRODUCTION SPECIALIST: KATHY MCCOLLEY
THE ILLUSTRATIONS IN THIS BOOK WERE CREATED DIGITALLY.

PICTURE WINDOW BOOKS
1710 ROE CREST DRIVE
NORTH MANKATO, MN 56003
WWW.CAPSTONEPUB.COM

LIBRARY OF CONGRESS CATALOGING-IN-PUBLICATION DATA
CATALOGING-IN-PUBLICATION INFORMATION IS ON FILE WITH THE LIBRARY OF CONGRESS.
ISBN 978-1-4048-7942-3 (LIBRARY BINDING)
ISBN 978-1-4048-8076-4 (PAPER OVER BOARD)
ISBN 978-1-4795-1885-2 (EBOOK PDF)

Printed in the United States of America in
North Mankato, Minnesota.
062013   007554R

# DIRECTIONS:

Look at the pictures and find the items on the lists. Not too tough, right? Not for a clever kid like you. But be warned: The first few puzzles are tricky. The next ones are even trickier. And the final puzzles are for the bravest seekers only. Good luck!

# TABLE OF CONTENTS

Happy Birthday!..............................4

Fútbol Aliencano.............................6

Alien Vacation...............................8

At the Movies...............................10

Keep Cool..................................12

Flight School...............................14

Alien Rock Star.............................16

Thrills and Chills..........................18

Get to Work................................20

Read It....................................22

Traffic Jam................................24

Auto Shop..................................26

Run!.......................................28

Campout....................................30

SAY WHAT?..................................32

Internet Sites.............................32

# Happy Birthday!

- cow
- bike
- cupcake
- kitten
- book
- moose

4

# Fútbol Aliencano

- football
- bowling pin
- baseball
- tennis racket
- hockey stick
- volleyball

# Alien Vacation

- cactus
- starfish
- moon
- hammer
- tomato
- loon

9

# At the Movies

-  raccoon
- crow
- bow tie
- newspaper
- banana
- mouse

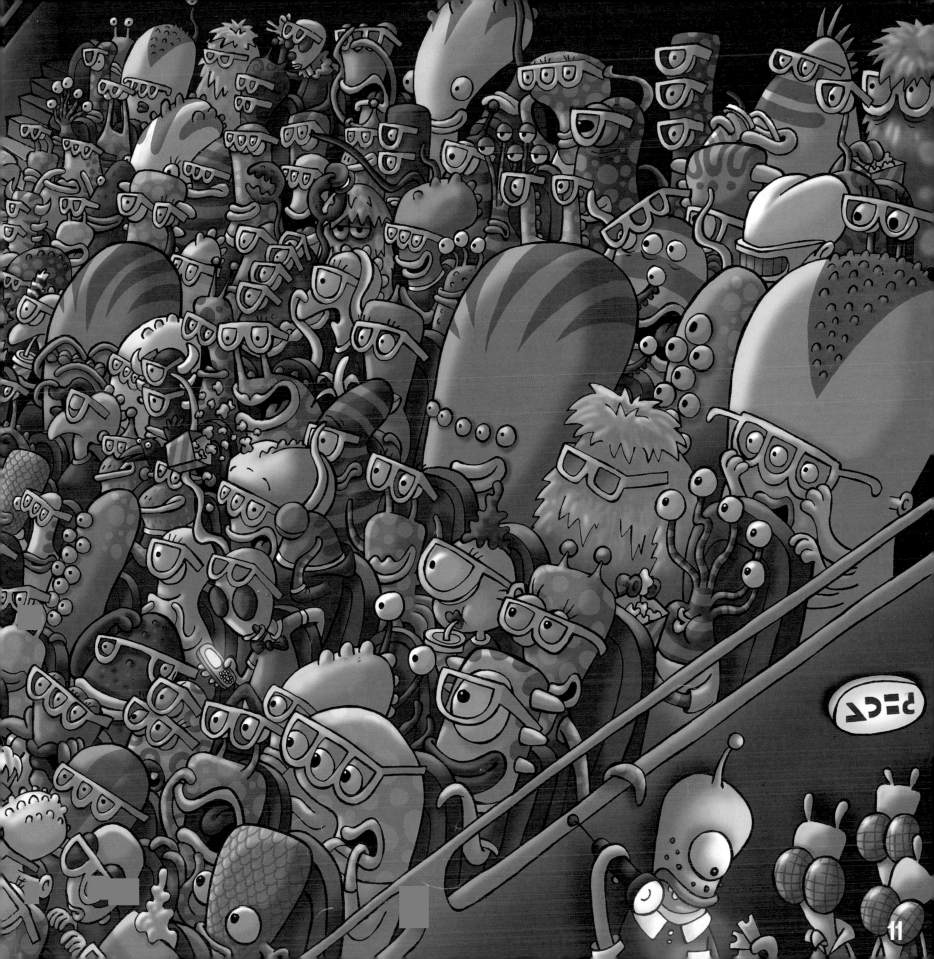

# Keep Cool

candy cane

lemon

duck

polar bear

Popsicle

seal

puppy

sunscreen

ice cube

Margaret E. Heggan Public
606 Delsea Drive
Sewell, NJ

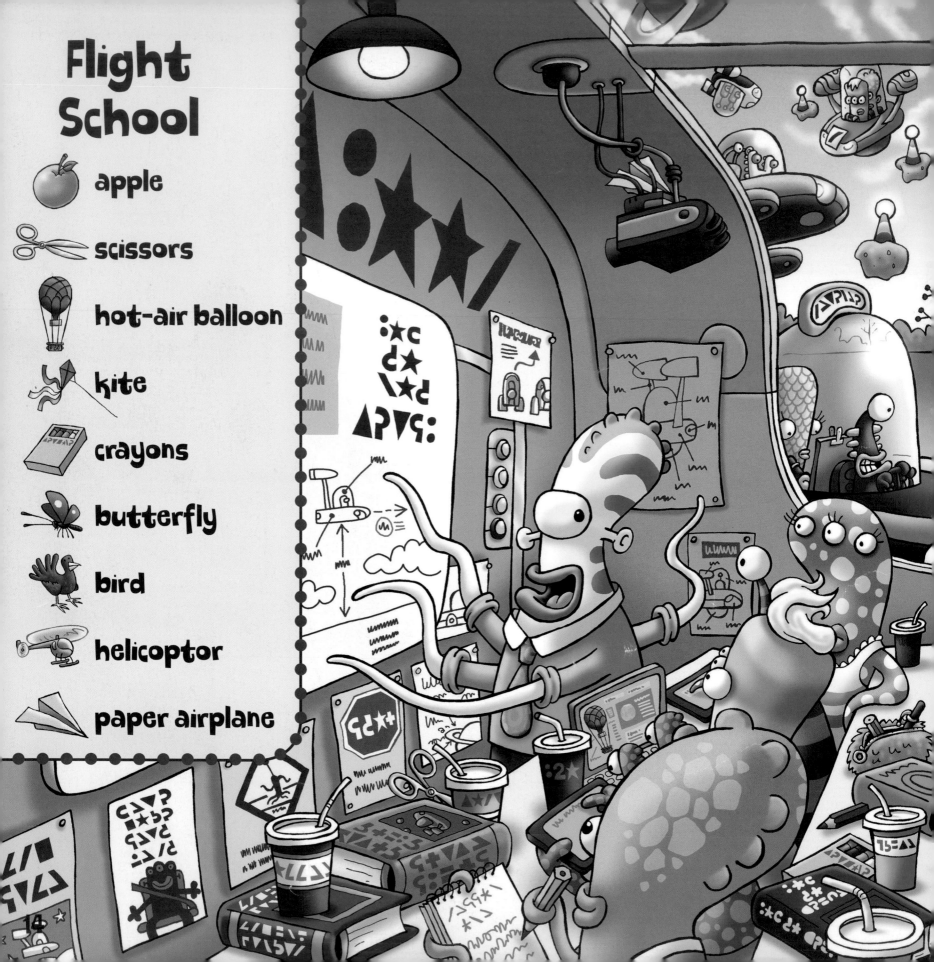

# Flight School

- apple
- scissors
- hot-air balloon
- kite
- crayons
- butterfly
- bird
- helicoptor
- paper airplane

15

# Alien Rock Star

- drum
- saxophone
- trombone
- violin
- harmonica
- harp
- flute
- tuba
- trumpet

# Thrills and Chills

- goose
- spider
- pretzel
- tie
- dollar bill
- comb
- lollipop
- bee
- shark

# Get to Work

- rooster
- bagel
- pencil
- picnic basket
- lobster
- soda can
- ant
- worm
- headphones

# Read It

 piggy bank

 wishbone

 toaster

 bull

 whale

 shell

 spoon

 watermelon

 hummingbird

 igloo

 butterfly

magnet

# Traffic Jam

 pizza

 banana

 photo

 pig

 gift

 cherries

 crayon

 yo-yo

 soccer ball

 beach ball

 octopus

 snail

# Auto Shop

 stoplight

 juice box

 lightbulb

 Earth

 soup can

 license plate

 clock

 flag

 gloves

 old tire

 pennant

 donut

26

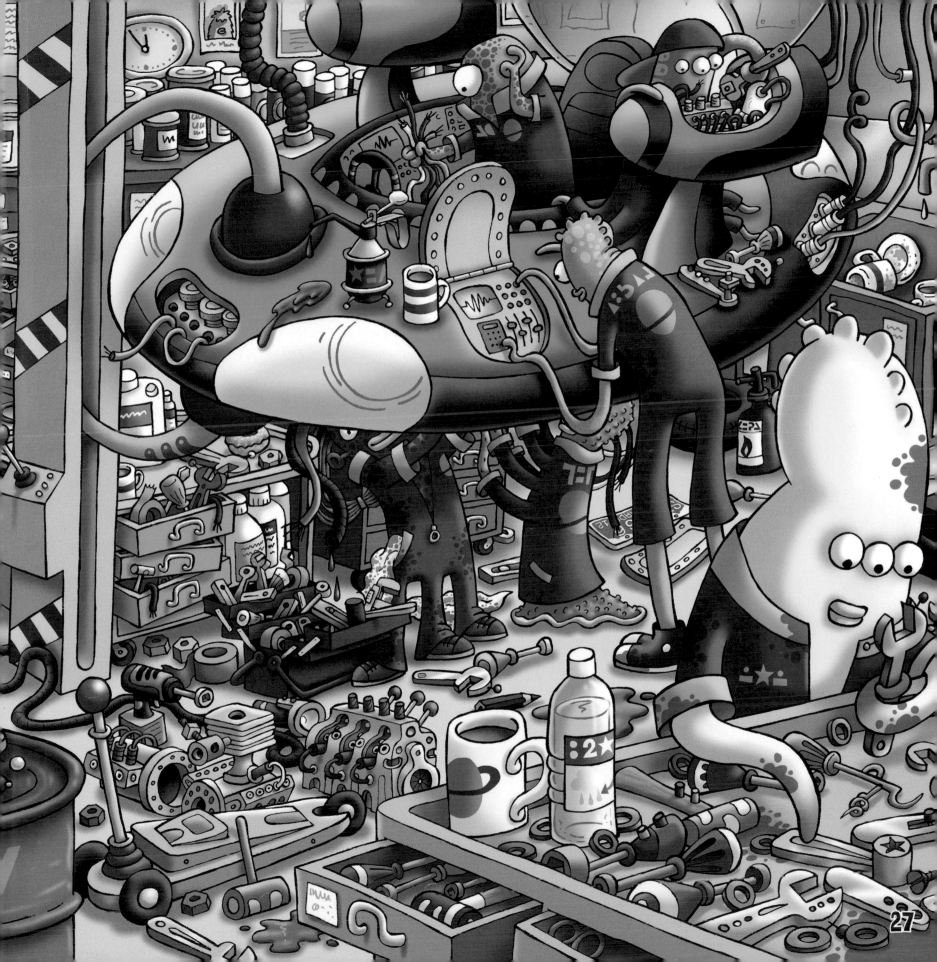

# Run!

 chicken

 stopwatch

 tennis ball

 lucky clover

 turtle

 tuba

 stamp

 teddy bear

 clown

 broom

 playing card

 bull

29

# Campout

 flower

 bug spray

 sailboat

 flashlight

 owl

 toothbrush

 arrow

 hula hoop

 sleeping bag

 camera

 letter

 life ring

# SAY WHAT?

**Flip Back** and see if you can decode the alien words!

| ▼ | ⬤ | ▲ | ◗ | ◣ | ◤ | ⊤ | ⦂ |
|---|---|---|---|---|---|---|---|
| **A** | **B** | **C** | **D** | **E** | **F** | **G** | **H** |

| ⊟ | ⌐ | ⌐ | ⁄ | ⌐ | ◣ | ★ | ✚ | ⚡ |
|---|---|---|---|---|---|---|---|---|
| **I** | **J** | **K** | **L** | **M** | **N** | **O** | **P** | **Q** |

| ? | ⌐ | ⊐ | ⊔ | ∩ | ⊂ | ⊃ | ■ | ◆ |
|---|---|---|---|---|---|---|---|---|
| **R** | **S** | **T** | **U** | **V** | **W** | **X** | **Y** | **Z** |

## Internet Sites

FactHound offers a safe, fun way to find Internet sites related to this book. All of the sites on FactHound have been researched by our staff.

Here's all you do:

Visit *www.facthound.com*

Type in this code: 9781404879423

Check out projects, games and lots more at
**www.capstonekids.com**

## look for all the books in the series:

**CHRISTMAS CHAOS**

**HALLOWEEN HIDE AND SEEK**

**OUT-OF-THIS-WORLD ALIENS**

**Pretty Princess PARTY**

**SCHOOL SHAKE-UP**

**ZOO HIDEOUT**